Family Fun-Days

Great days out for everyone!

A round Britain regional guide to fun days out for all the family!

(im)PulsePaperbacks

This fabulous book is packed with ideas to keep all of the family - young and old - entertained. Lightweight enough for you to take on your holidays, the book travels around the regions of the UK looking at some of the best attractions. Whether you are planning weekend trips, half-term breaks or a summer getaway this book will hopefully inspire you and give you ideas you hadn't thought of.

Each entry gives a brief description of the attraction along with the address, the website (where you will find full details of the attraction) opening times and facilities on offer. As admission charges are subject to change, we have produced a price guide which is based on 2 adults and 2 children, but you should contact the attraction direct for exact prices. The book also includes some fantastic activities and attractions that are free to help you balance your holiday costs.

£ = Up to £15   **££ = Up to £30**   **£££ = £30 and over**

Have fun!

London

Natural History Museum
Cromwell Road, London, SW7 5BD
Free (charges may apply for certain exhibitions)

With hundreds of exciting and interactive exhibits, the Natural History Museum is one of the world's largest museums of natural history – and undoubtedly one of the best. The museum's impressive and unforgettable exhibits are divided into different sections: Zoology, Palaeontology, Botany, Mineralogy and Entomology! Highlights of the museum, which children will especially enjoy include: 'Creepy-Crawlies', 'Dinosaurs' and 'Human Biology' and not to be missed is the 'Mammals' section of the museum, with its awe-inspiring huge blue whale. The museum has a changing programme of special events, please check the official website for details.

Opening Times:
Daily, exc. 24 – 26 Dec. 10am to 5.50pm
www.nhm.ac.uk

Facilities:
Disabled full, guided tour, refreshments, café, restaurant, shop

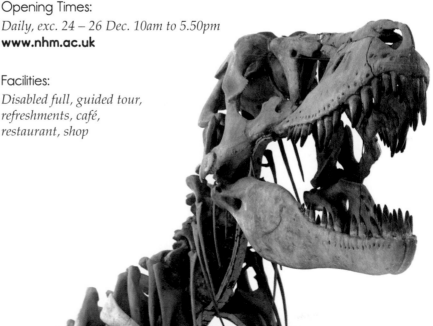

Madame Tussauds

Marleybone Road, London, NW1 5LR
£££

Constantly changing its famous exhibits, Madame Tussauds is certainly one way to get up close and personal with the rich and famous! Whether it be Brad Pitt, Nicole Kidman, J-Lo or the latest James Bond the whole family will enjoy the remarkable life-size waxwork models. You can take a look behind the scenes and find out how the figures are made.

Opening Times:
All year, exc. 25 Dec. All weekends and UK school holidays, 9am to 6pm. Off-peak weekdays 9.30am to 5.30pm
www.madametussauds.com

Facilities:
Disabled access; please telephone in advance for booking 0870 400 3000, café, gift shop

British Museum

Great Russell Street, London, WC1B 3DG
Free

Visitors to one of the world's finest museum will be blown-away by the range and quality of its displays, sculptures and special exhibitions. Housing displays of antiquities from as far back as Roman and Medieval Britain, there are also worldwide exhibits. The museum offers a range of audio tours, and is an excellent information-rich and fascinating visit for all the family.

Opening Times:
Daily, 10am to 5.30pm – Open late Thursday & Friday
www.britishmuseum.org

Facilities:
Disabled full, guided tours, refreshments, café, shop, restaurant

London Eye

Westminster Bridge Road, London, SE1 7PB
£££

Synonymous with the centre of London, this stunning and popular attraction is an absolute must-see for visitors wanting to take in London's most celebrated landmarks. The London Eye draws in visitors from far and wide. The tallest observation wheel in the world, its guests are taken on a gradual 30 minute ride high above Londons sights.

Opening Times:
Daily, exc. 25 Dec. Check website for cleaning closure dates. October to April, 10am to 8pm. May to September, 10am to 9pm daily (July & August open until 9.30pm) **www.londoneye.com**

Facilities:
Disabled full. Children's playground, shops & cafés all at ground level

Tower of London

Tower Hill, London, EC3N 4AB
£££

Take yourself back through 1,000 years of history at one of the world's most famous fortresses which holds in its walls the sparkling beauty of the Crown. Take part in the family trails and the guided tours and in events hosted throughout the year; please check official website for details.

Opening Times:
Times vary throughout the year, please check website for details
www.hrp.org.uk/toweroflondon

Facilities:
Disabled limited, guided tours, shop, café, restaurant

ZSL London Zoo
Regent's Park, London, NW1 4RY
£££

Situated in the leafy surroundings of Regent's Park, London Zoo boasts its historical first as the world's first scientific zoo. Housing over 650 species of animals, there are many that you won't be able to see anywhere else in the UK. To recreate the perfect settings, you will experience the sights, sounds and smells of rainforests and tropical climates. Gorilla Kingdom allows visitors to take a walk-through for a close-up look at their group of Western Lowland Gorillas and you can see wonders such as tamarinds, marmosets and many other forest dwellers in another part of the zoo. There's an exciting daily programme of events and displays, including feeds and expert talks. A fabulous day out for animal enthusiasts of all ages!

Opening Times:
Summer opening daily, 10am to 5.30pm. For winter opening please see website in season **www.zsl.org/zsl-london-zoo**

Facilities:
Disabled full, shop, café, refreshments, restaurant, parking

Peter Harrison Planetarium
Royal Observatory, Blackheath Avenue, Greenwich, SE10 8XJ
Please check website for prices

Housed at the Royal Observatory, this fabulous planetarium opened in 2007 is the centre of the Royal Observatory site. Inside the cone is Europe's first digital laser planetarium projector, making possible shows which take the audiences out into space looking back at Earth, as well as the inclusion of up-to-the-minute images sent back by space probes.

Opening Times:
The Royal Observatory is open daily, 10am - 5pm. Last admission 4.30pm. Last planetarium show 4:00pm. Closed 24-26 December.

Facilities:
Check website for details
www.nmm.ac.uk

Leeds Castle & Gardens

Maidstone, Kent, ME17 1PL

£££

Rising regally from two islands in the centre of a lake, Leeds Castle is known as 'the loveliest castle in the world'. Historically home to six of the Medieval queens of England and a royal palace of King Henry VIII, it's history spans more than 1,000 years. As well as the beautiful tapestries, furnishings and antiques within the castle, there are 500 acres of parkland and gardens to explore and enjoy. Guided tours are available and other attractions include a duckery and aviary, a beautiful woodland walk, a spiralling Yew maze, greenhouses and a vineyard and an underworld grotto, with carved mythical beasts. Younger visitors can enjoy a huge adventure playground, a craft centre and t-shirt painting activities.

Opening Times:
Times vary for castle & grounds and seasons, please see website for details
www.leeds-castle.com

Facilities:
Disabled access, guided tours, restaurant, audio tour hire

The Royal Pavilion

4/5 Pavilion Buildings, Brighton, East Sussex BN1 1EE

£££

An exquisite and exotically striking building, the Royal Pavilion was the one-time famous seaside palace of King George IV. The Pavilion's aesthetics are in the most striking Indian style, with dramatic colours, fabrics and furnishings. The craftsmanship is nothing but superb.

The Music Room has a striking domed ceiling and the Banqueting Room is beautifully lit by a chandelier, held by a silvered dragon. The true beauty of this building can only be truly appreciated by visiting it and taking in its scenic delights!

Opening Times:
Daily, exc. 25 & 26 Dec. October to March 10am to 5.15pm. April to September 9.30am to 5.45pm
www.royalpavilion.org.uk

Facilities:
Disabled limited, audio tours, café

Legoland Windsor

Winkfield Road, Windsor, Buckinghamshire, SL4 4AY

£££

A unique and whole day of fantastic family-fun! Based around seven main activity areas, Legoland is home to hundreds of fascinating models, more than 40 rides, live shows and attractions and plenty of fun activities. Step inside the Land of the Vikings; take the Orient Expedition, a train ride that will take you across exotic landscapes full of wild animals; and take a fascinating journey through the Explorer's Institute and find the seven magic keys! Bounded by beautiful extensive parkland and gardens, visitors can take time out of the activities and relax in the scenic surroundings.

Opening Times:
Times vary throughout the year, please see website for details **www.legoland.co.uk**

Facilities:
Disabled access, parking, shop, café, refreshments, restaurant

Chessington World of Adventures

Leatherhead Road, Chessington, Surrey, KT9 2NE

£££

A real all-round family attraction, Chessington World of Adventures offers an exciting range of rides, games, animals and adventures! Animal lovers will delight at 'Animal Land', where visitors can meet Europe's most successful West Lowland Gorilla families. Children will love 'Beanoland' where they can meet the characters of the Beano gang. There's the mysterious and slightly scary 'Forbidden Kingdom' and the 'Land of the Dragons' where visitors can venture into the Dragon's lair – if they dare!

Opening Times:
Times vary throughout the year, please see website for details
www.chessington.com

Facilities:
Disabled limited, see website for full details. Parking, shop, café, refreshments, restaurant

Beaulieu (National Motor Museum)

National Motor Museum, Beaulieu, Brockenhurst, Hampshire, SO45 5DT

£££

Home of the National Motor Museum, Beaulieu hosts an impressive and unique display of over 250 vehicles, with world record breaking vehicles such as the legendary Bluebird and Golden Arrow – and the James Bond Experience, with a selection of vehicles used within the films. There are motoring events organised throughout the year, please see website for details.

Opening Times:
Daily, exc. 25 Dec. October to May, 10am to 5pm. May to September, 10am to 6pm
www.beaulieu.co.uk

Didcot Railway Centre

Great Western Society, Didcot, Oxfordshire, OX11 7NJ

££/£££

A living museum of the Great Western Railway situated around its original site, the Didcot Railway Centre is home to an impressive collection of steam locomotives, wagons and carriages. The centre has 'Steamdays' when the locomotives are brought back into use and visitors can have the rare treat of riding in these historic 1930's trains; an experience not to be missed!

Opening Times:
Times vary throughout the year, please see website for details
www.didcotrailwaycentre.org.uk

Facilities:
Disabled limited, shop, café, dogs on leads

Roman Baths

Pump Room, Stall Street, Bath, BA1 1LZ
£££

A popular West Country attraction, the Roman Baths is an incredibly well-preserved Roman site containing the remains of one of the most famous religious and finest thermal spas of the ancient world. Stunning by day, or by night; there's a superb Roman Museum and of course, the fabulous historic baths with their hot temperatures and thousands of gallons of water. A historically fascinating and interesting visit for all the family, children are provided with an interactive audio-guide – and there are costumed characters on show every afternoon, bringing history to life and giving these ancient baths an even more authentic feel.

Opening Times:
Times vary throughout the year, please see website **www.romanbaths.co.uk**

Facilities:
Disabled limited, guided tours, shop, restaurant

Cheddar Caves & Gorge

Cheddar, Somerset, BS27 3QF
£££

These fascinating and famous caves at Cheddar Gorge boast being the region's most popular attractions. Take a guided tour through the caves and find out about their formation and discovery. These caves also fired the imagination of JRR Tolkien, author of the trilogy "Lord of the Rings", on his honeymoon visit in 1916. See the amazing stalagmites and stalactites in Gough's Cave; take part in the Crystal Quest Challenge, an underground fantasy adventure game and meet the Cheddar Man, Britain's oldest complete skeleton! During the summer months there's an open-top bus tour for visitors to take in the breathtaking surroundings and a cliff-top walk.

Opening Times:
Daily, exc. 24 & 25 Dec. July & August, 10am to 5.30pm. Remaining part of the year, 10.30am to 5pm
www.cheddarcaves.co.uk

Corfe Castle

The Square, Wareham, Dorset, BH20 5EZ
££

Surrounded by beautiful countryside and panoramic views, this famous ruined castle has a wealth of fascinating history to discover and explore. Corfe Castle has stood as a fortress, a prison and a home throughout its existence and the Castle View Visitor Centre charts its story through the ages with hands on displays and original castle artefacts. Children are actively encouraged to engage with the castle's history and can have great fun trying on authentic-looking replica medieval clothing! The castle holds various children's activities throughout the holidays; as well as organising special events such as the bringing to life of historical events with fantastic re-enactments, please contact direct on 01929 481294 for further details.

Opening Times:
Times vary, please see website
www.nationaltrust.org.uk

Facilities:
Shop, café

Durdle Door & Lulworth Cove
Lulworth Cove, Dorset

Durdle Door in Dorset with its massive rock arch, set right on the Jurassic Coast between Swanage and Weymouth, is absolutely beautiful. Just along the coast path from Lulworth Cove with its thatched cottages, fishing boats, lobster pots, wild flowers, quaint gift shops and tea rooms - the charm of the place is timeless and you will want to return again and again. The World Heritage Committee of UNESCO has assessed the superb coastline for the award of World Heritage Site status because its geology and physical geography is of international conservation importance. Don't miss it!

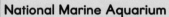

National Marine Aquarium
Rope Walk, Coxside, Plymouth, Devon, PL4 0LF
£££/Children under 4 – Free

Britain's biggest and Europe's deepest aquarium, the National Marine Aquarium is a must-see attraction. Bringing the fascinating world of the oceans deepest wonders to its visitors, this awe-inspiring aquarium with its incredible reefs and coral kingdoms, is home to the most exotic and amazing sea creatures in the world. Dedicated to conservation issues, education and research this experience will delight, inform and inspire you.

Opening Times:
Daily. April to October, 10am to 6pm. November to March, 10am to 5pm
www.national-aquarium.co.uk

Facilities:
Disabled full, guided tours, shop, café, refreshments

Eden Project

Bodelva, St Austell, Cornwall,
PL24 2SG

£££

Visit the largest greenhouses in the world at this remarkable and awe inspiring attraction. Eden Project is home to a world of plants from diverse habitats, such as tropical rainforests and Mediterranean fruit groves. Based on a site which boasts the size of 30 football pitches, there's a plethora of sights, colours, shapes and smells as far as the senses can see, smell and touch!

Opening Times:
Daily, exc. 24 & 25 Dec. March to October, 10am to 6pm. For winter opening times, please see website **www.edenproject.com**

Facilities:
Disabled full, parking, guided tours, shop, café, refreshments, restaurant

The Cornish Fishing Villages
From Boscastle, to Fowey, to Mevagissey, to Mousehole, to Polperro - the beautiful cornish fishing villages offer visitors an architectural step into the past with steep winding streets crammed with quaint houses, shops and restaurants. Each village has its own unique charm so indulge your senses with a trip to the cornish coast - not forgetting to sample the famous local cuisine!

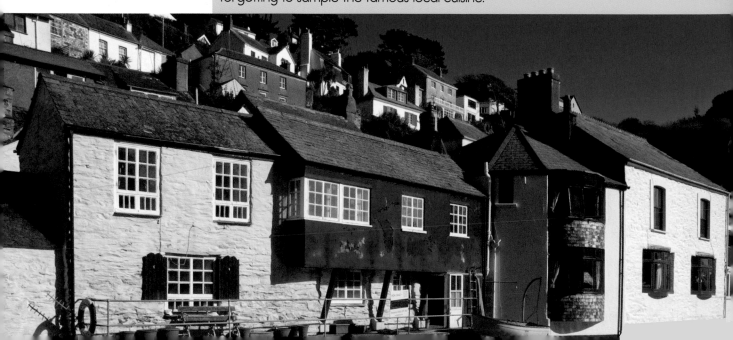

Cotswold Farm Park

Guiting Power, Cheltenham, Gloucestershire, GL54 5UG
££

Animal lovers of all ages will enjoy the charm of Cotswold Farm Park and its appreciation of conservational and educational issues. This unique attraction is home to rare breeds of British farm animals, with over 50 herds in beautiful surroundings. The park's living historical collection of rare breeds includes; cattle, sheep, goats, pigs, poultry, waterfowl and horses. There are indoor and outdoor animal displays, a farm nature trail, farm safari ride, a 2-mile wildlife walk and an indoor tractor school.

Opening Times:
Daily, March – September, 10.30am to 5.00pm.
Please check the website for autumn/winter opening times.
www.cotsworldfarmpark.co.uk

Facilities:
Disabled full, gift shop, café

Warwick Castle

Warwick, Warwickshire, CV34 4QU
£££

Visit Warwick Castle and experience over 1,000 years of history. Situated upon the River Avon the Castle has many areas of interest with its beautiful rooms and furniture, battlements and scenic views. See the Medieval preparation for battle in 'Kingmaker', scare yourself in the Ghost Tower, join a Victorian Royal Weekend Party and explore the dungeons of the Castle. There are picnic areas for visitors to enjoy eating outdoors, with special events throughout the year, including jousting and medieval markets. Please see the official website for details of events:
www.warwick-castle.co.uk

Opening Times:
Daily, exc. 25 Dec. January to March, 10.00am to 5.00pm, April to September, 10.00am to 6.00pm, October to December, 10.00am to 5.00pm.

Facilities:
Disabled limited, café, refreshments, gift shop

Cadbury World

Linden Road, Bourneville, Birmingham, B30 2LU
£££

Great fun for the family – and anyone who enjoys chocolate! Enjoy 'Cadabra' a magical Cadbury journey and the Cadbury Fantasy Factory. Visitors will learn about making chocolate, where it came from and when, who made it and first drank it and when it was first enjoyed as a solid. Discover the true history of Cadbury, tracing back to the ancient Maya and Aztec civilisations. There are events and entertainment programmes throughout the year, please see website for details.

Opening Times:
Daily, times may vary throughout the year. See website for details
www.cadburyworld.co.uk

Facilities:
Disabled full, (some area restrictions apply on health and safety grounds), guide dogs welcome, parking, shop, café, restaurant

Alton Towers

Alton, Stoke-on-Trent, Staffordshire, ST10 4DB
£££/Children under 4 – Free

For thrill-seekers and adrenaline junkies, Alton Towers plays host to legendary white-knuckle rides such as Oblivion, Air, Nemesis and Rita – Queen of Speed. For younger family members, the park has a large area of rides dedicated to toddlers and small children. Families can enjoy the water-rides such as the Rapids and the Log Flume. For those who want a more relaxing experience travel on the air-lift over the expanse of the park or take a boat ride on one of the lakes. Priority passes can be purchased to bypass queues for the main attractions, and pre-booking via the website allows you to book family packages. See website for details **www.altontowers.com**

Opening Times:
Daily. Mid-March to November from 9.30am. Closing times vary throughout the season. Please see official website for details.

Facilities:
Disabled access, wheelchair hire, luggage lockers, gift shops, café, restaurant, refreshments

Chatsworth House & Garden

Chatsworth House, Bakewell, DE45 1PP

££

Situated in the heart of the Derbyshire Peak District, Chatsworth House is one of Britain's most famous and beautifully maintained historic houses. As well as its obvious aesthetic beauty, Chatsworth offers a fabulous range of attractions for all the family. Chatsworth's grounds play host to beautiful water features, including the famous Cascade, recently voted England's best water feature. There are 5 miles of walks, a huge maze and children can enjoy meeting the animals in the farmyard and expending lots of energy in the adventure playground. Dogs on leads are welcome for the grounds only.

Opening Times:
Daily, 15 March to 23 December, 11.00am to 6.00pm
www.chatsworth.org

Facilities:
Disabled access, guide dogs welcome, gift shops, café, restaurant

Rutland Water

Sykes Lane, Empingham, Rutland, LE15 8PX

A fabulous destination and great day out for the whole family, Rutland Water encompasses a 3,100 acre lake. With over 20 miles of off-road cycling or walking, its surroundings are beautifully serene. Perfect for picnics and taking in the scenery, try out the nature reserve, museum and butterfly and aquatic centre. For a more active visit, visitors can hire bicycles on site, take part in the various watersports available, or have a go on the climbing wall. For a more sedate experience perhaps indulge in a spot of fishing.

Opening Times:
All year, except 25 December. Times vary throughout the year, please see website for details; **www.rutlandwater.org.uk**

Sherwood Pines Forest Park & Visitor Centre

Forestry Commission, Edwinstowe, Nottingham, NG21 9JL

Sherwood Pines Forest Park is set in the heart of the ancient and legendary Sherwood Forest. The park is the largest woodland open to the general public in the East Midlands, offering a wildlife haven and beautiful walking and cycling routes for all ages to enjoy. The visitor centre provides cycle hire, refreshments and sales of interest to the area. There is an off-road area marked especially for mountain bikes. The park also hosts open air concerts during the summer months.

Opening Times:
Daily, exc. 25 Dec. Call 0845 3673787 for details **www.forestry.gov.uk**

Facilities:
Disabled access, café, refreshments, restaurant, shop

Shepreth Wildlife Park

Station Road, Shepreth, Nr Royston, SG8 6PZ

££

After first starting out as a private wildlife sanctuary in 1979, Shepreth Wildlife Park has grown into a fabulous wildlife park, giving homes to many adopted animals ranging from exotic animals from zoos that have closed down, road accident victims and orphans. Children will delight at celebrating the annual Tiger's Tea Party! A wonderful testament to kindness to animals and a must-see for animal lovers of all ages.

Opening Times:
Closed 25 December. Summer/Autumn 10.00am to 6.00pm; Winter/Spring 10.00am to Dusk.
www.sheprethwildlifepark.co.uk

Facilities:
Disabled limited, shop, café, refreshments

Imperial War Museum Duxford

Cambridge, CB22 4QR

££/15 years and under free

Come and relive life during the two World Wars at Europe's premier aviation Museum, standing on an original wartime airfield. This collection of military vehicles, tanks, artillery, and other military exhibits is also home to 200 aircraft, including Concorde, Lancaster and of course, the mighty Spitfire. Visitors can walk through the trenches and experience the sights and sounds and smells of London during an air raid, sharing in the dramatic Blitz experience. The American Air Museum houses the carefully restored B-24 Liberator and hosts the largest collection of US aircraft outside of America. The museum hosts annual air shows and many other events. Please see the official website for details:
www.iwm.org.uk

Opening Times:
Daily exc. 24 – 26 Dec. March to Oct 10am to 6pm. Oct to March, 10am to 4pm

Facilities:
Disabled full, parking, shop, café, refreshments, restaurant

Nene Valley Railway

Wansford Station, Stibbington, Peterborough, PE8 6LR

£££

Hosting an impressive collection of British and continental locomotives and carriages, the Nene Valley Railway is a great day out for all ages. Boasting the last surviving coach from the Great Train Robbery of 1963 and the carefully restored Southern Railway Travelling Post Office carriage, for younger visitors it's also

home to 'Thomas', the famous children's favourite tank engine! There is a small museum and second-hand railway bookshop. Some of the carriages and locomotives are still in use and visitors can travel between Wansford and Peterborough, through the centre of the beautiful Ferry Meadows Country Park. Special events are organised throughout the year and Santa Specials run throughout December for children, (and for those who still love Christmas!)

Opening Times:
Times vary throughout the year. Please check website for details:
www.nvr.org.uk

Facilities:
Disabled full, parking, guided tours, sales point, shop, café, refreshments

Norfolk & Suffolk Broads
Broads Authority, 18 Colegate, Norwich,
NR3 1BQ

As Britain's largest protected wetland, the Norfolk and Suffolk Broads have been one of England's most popular holiday areas since Edwardian times. With its exquisite scenery, the Broads provide 125 miles of waterways and navigable routes, rich in habitat for broadland wildlife in their grazing marshes, fields and woodlands. The Broads are especially noted for their churches, rare wildlife and plants, and their stunning windmills. Visitors can choose to hire a boat or remain on land, taking in the beautiful sights and walking along the public footpaths.

Information:
www.norfolkbroads.com

Great Yarmouth Pleasure Beach
South Beach Parade, Great Yarmouth,
Norfolk, NR30 3EH

Situated on the seafront at the southern end of Great Yarmouth's famed Golden Mile, the Pleasure Beach hosts an impressive 70+ rides, water attractions, arcades and two crazy golf courses. Children of all ages will love the thrill of the sights and sounds of the rides, stalls and activities – all the fun of the fair at the seaside! Adults can take advantage of the gardens for a bit of well deserved rest and relaxation.

Opening Times:
Opening times vary and can be subject to weather conditions. Please visit the official website for details:
www.pleasure-beach.co.uk

Yorkshire

Yorkshire Dales

With some of the most beautiful and unique scenery in the world, the Yorkshire Dales are a fabulous day out for all of the family. With spectacular walking, cycling and riding, the Yorkshire Dales is an outdoor paradise with valleys, crags, peaks, caves and moorlands that stretch over 1,600 square miles. Hidden among the amazing scenery lie many traditional vibrant market towns offering a vast array of shops offering beautiful crafts, located alongside markets selling fine local produce from Yorkshire farmers. Throughout the summer the Yorkshire Dales come alive with festivals, galas and shows and whether you want fun and adventure or culture and tranquillity you will find it all in the Yorkshire Dales.

Visit **www.yorkshiredales.org** to plan your trip and for more detailed information on particular areas and towns.

Fountains Abbey

Fountains, Ripon, HG4 3DY
£££

Situated in the scenic landscape of Ripon in North Yorkshire, this outstanding historic Abbey and gardens offer a prefect day out to enjoy the scenery and take in the peace of its surroundings. Attractions include the Medieval Deer Park, Georgian Water Garden, and Elizabethan Hall and Victorian Church. Children can enjoy the gardens, wildlife walks and during the school holidays there are special events and exhibitions, including the children's theatre. Evening events include open air Shakespeare in the summer and floodlit evenings in the autumn.

Opening Times
Daily, exc. 24 & 25 Dec. March to Oct 10am to 5pm. Nov to Feb 10am to 4pm. Closes at dusk if earlier.
www.fountainsabbey.org.uk

Facilities:
Disabled full, parking, guided tours, shop, café, refreshments, restaurant

Skipton Castle

Skipton, North Yorkshire, BD23 1AW
££

Over 900 years old and despite having endured a three year siege during the Civil War, Skipton Castle is one of the most well preserved medieval castles in England. Inside its walls there is the charming Tudor Courtyard, the grand Banqueting Hall, the Kitchen, the Bedchamber, and even the Privy! Visitors can climb the castle from the depths of its Dungeon to the top of its Watch Tower. Enjoy a walk in nearby Skipton woods and soak up the peace and beautiful scenery, or take a picnic into the grounds of the castle. The castle holds events throughout the year.
www.skiptoncastle.co.uk

Opening Times:
Daily, exc. 25 Dec. 10am to 6pm (Closes at 4pm October to February)

Facilities:
Guided tours, shop, café, refreshments

Roundhay Park

Roundhay Park, Princes Avenue, Leeds, LS8 2ER

Situated in 700 acres of winning parkland, Roundhay Park and Tropical World is a wonderful family day out. Spend your time exploring the park's woodland, lakes, impressive parklands and flowering gardens. Find the castle folly and discover the re-interpretation of famous gardens.

Opening Times:
Please see website for details
www.roundhaypark.org.uk

Facilities:
Disabled full, parking, shop, refreshments

Robin Hood's Bay

Nr Whitby, North Yorkshire

Whether you are on a day trip or a weekly holiday to Robin Hood's Bay, finishing a coast to coast tour or simply getting away from it all, there is much to indulge in and certainly something for everyone. In addition to simply soaking up the scenery and relaxing in the surroundings, let your taste buds be tickled and your creative side tempted! The area has beautiful wildlife, fauna and flora and historic buildings, streets and cobbled pathways.

JORVIK Viking Centre
Coppergate, York, YO1 9WT
£££

Journey back in time to the very heart of York as it would have been in AD975! On a visit to this unique and fascinating site, JORVIK offers its visitors the opportunity to come face-to-face with Vikings on an original Viking site; and discover what life was like over 1,000 years ago. Experience the sights, sounds and even the smells of the Viking era in a faithful reconstruction of a Viking-age street. Even the faces of the models you'll see have been reconstructed from Viking skulls! Check out the exhibition; 'Are You a Viking?'

Opening Times:
Daily, exc. 24 to 26 Dec. 10am to 5pm
www.jorvik-viking-centre.co.uk

Facilities:
Disabled full, guided tours, sales point, shop, café, refreshments

National Railway Museum
Leeman Road, York, YO26 4XJ
Free

As the largest railway museum in the world, there's plenty to see at the National Railway Museum. With three huge galleries, filled with fun, knowledge and interesting exhibits you can discover the story of the train, told by the historical engines, photos, documents, pictures and the millions of incredible artefacts. The museum is home to over 100 engines, from the world's fastest locomotive to the modern-day Eurostar; from Japanese Bullet trains to Queen Victoria's favourite carriage.

Opening Times:
Daily, exc. 24 to 26 Dec. 10am to 6pm
www.nrm.org.uk

Facilities:
Disabled full, guided tours, parking, sales point, shop, café, refreshments, restaurant

York Minster
York Minster, Deangate, York, YO1 7JF
££

Boasting the title of the largest Gothic cathedral in Northern Europe, this stunning landmark is home to some of the most beautiful fourteenth and fifteenth century stained glass windows in the world. With nearly 1,000 years of history, the Undercroft and Crypt is privy to the history of York Minster, from its beginnings in Norman times to the modern-day engineering that we see today, with its remarkable support of the central tower. Take an audio-tour to hear the stories of the Minster and its ceremonial beauty.

Opening Times:
Check website for details
www.yorkminster.org

Facilities:
Guided tours, shop, café, refreshments

Hack Green Secret Bunker
Nantwich, Cheshire, CW5 8AL
££

A real-life government nuclear war headquarters, fully equipped with searchlights and fighter aircraft control, this bunker was a secret for over 50 years! Built in the 1950's and converted in the 1980's, to accommodate the Cold War's threat of nuclear attack, this underground museum contains remarkable equipment, previously unseen by the general public.

Opening Times:
Please see website for details
www.hackgreen.co.uk

Facilities:
Blind/partially sighted facilities, deaf/hearing impaired facilities, guided tours, shop ,refreshments, parking

The Lake District Visitor Centre
Brockhole, Windermere, Cumbria, LA23 1LJ
Free

Located in an Edwardian house on the shores of the beautiful Lake Windermere in the ever-popular Lake District, the Visitor Centre is a superb way to spend a day with all the family. There are fabulous landscaped gardens, stunning views, guided walks, lake tours, great interactive exhibitions, picnic area and an adventure playground. There are special events organised throughout the year, please check website for details.

Opening Times:
Times and dates vary, please see website
www.lake-district.gov.uk

Facilities:
Disabled full, parking, gift shop, café, refreshments

Beamish, Open Air Museum
Beamish, Durham, DH9 0RG
££/£££ Seasonally

An extraordinary day out for family members of all ages, this multi award-winning museum boasts being Britain's favourite open-air museum. Located in over 300 acres of picturesque countryside this popular 'living' attraction depicts life in the north of England in the early 1800's and 1900's. Visitors can touch, taste, smell and experience the past.

Opening Times:
Daily, March to November 10am to 5pm. For winter opening times, see website
www.beamish.org.uk

Facilities:
Disabled limited, parking, shop, café, refreshments

The Blackpool Piers

Blackpool Piers, Blackpool

With each of the 3 Blackpool Piers having its own attractions, atmosphere and character – there's something for all members of the family to enjoy. The North Pier boasts the best view of Blackpool's promenade and annual illuminations; with an original Venetian carousel ride and the aptly named, Carousel Bar visitors can take in a more nostalgic and relaxing view of Blackpool. The family-friendly Central Pier features an amusement area, with rides and attractions for younger members of the family. The South Pier is fondly coined as the 'Adrenaline Pier' and is THE place for all thrill-seekers, with white-knuckle rides a-plenty – not for those of a nervous disposition!

The World of Glass

Chalon Way East, St Helens, Merseyside, WA10 1BX
££

Watch the centre's glassblowers create fantastic and creative shaped pieces before your eyes – and watch in wonder as they expertly wield the fascinating tools of this ancient craft. Children can have great fun exploring the maze of tunnels and there's a fun-zone with distorting mirrors and kaleidoscopes.

Opening Times:
Exc. 25 & 26 Dec, 1 Jan. Tues to Sun (& Bank Holidays), 10am to 5pm

Facilities:
Disabled full, parking, sales point, shop, café, refreshments

Alnwick Castle

Alnwick, Northumberland, NE66 1NQ
£££

This captivating eleventh century castle is a beautiful example of magnificent English heritage and children will recognize it from the Harry Potter films. Inside its walls are Italian Renaissance furnishings, local archaeology and beautiful art exhibits. Enjoy exploring the extensive and beautiful grounds; children can try Dragon's Quest where they'll face challenges and solve dark mysteries of the castle and caverns

Opening Times:
Daily, March to October, Grounds: 10am to 6pm. Castle: 11am to 5pm. For winter opening times, please see website for details **www.alnwickcastle.com**

Facilities:
Disabled limited in some areas – please see website for details. Guide dogs welcome, parking, guided tours, shop, café, refreshments, restaurant

Souter Lighthouse

Coast Road, Whitburn, Sunderland, Tyne & Wear SR6 7NH
££/Children under 4 – Free

This striking Victorian lighthouse was the world's first electric lighthouse. With breathtaking views over Marsden Bay and the notorious currents of 'Whitburn Steel' the lighthouse provides hands-on activities for all the family.

Opening Times:
Times vary throughout the year, please see website **www.nationaltrust.org.uk**

Facilities:
Disabled, parking, picnic area, shop, café, refreshments, tea-room

Wales

Heart of Wales Line

Llangennech, Llanelli, SA14 8TG
Prices vary, please see website

This Heart of Wales of Line Form is one of Britain's finest scenic routes; spanning across tranquil and picturesque villages, Victorian Spa towns, winding rivers, sprawling hills, panoramic views of the countryside and stunning estuaries. Visitors will be in awe of the scenery and natural beauty; whether young or old, toddler or teen. A favourite of seasoned travellers, make this one of your must-see sights in the heart of the Wales countryside.

Opening Times:
Times vary, please see website for details
www.heart-of-wales.co.uk

Dolaucothi Gold Mines

Pumsaint, Llanwrda, Carmarthenshire, SA19 8US
££

Take a journey back in time to some latter day gold mines! Dating back to ancient Roman times, this mine was also a working mine in the nineteenth and twentieth centuries. You'll be taken on a fascinating underground guided tour of the mines and children and adults alike will have the opportunity to do some gold panning!

Opening Times:
March to November, 10am to 5pm. For winter opening times please see website for details in season
www.nationaltrust.org.uk

Facilities:
Shop, café, cycle hire

Felinwynt Butterfly Centre

Felinwynt, Cardigan, West Wales, SA3 1RT
££

Visitors will be treated to a tropical feast of exotic colours, sights and sounds in this excellent rainforest re-creation. With its spectacular tropical butterflies, lush plants, dramatic waterfalls and streams, the centre has much to offer; as well as other tropical wildlife such as birds, stick insects and the Leafcutter ants! Children will love getting up close and personal with the wildlife, as well as enjoying the art activities which are put on especially for them.

Opening Times:
Daily. March to September, 10.30am to 5pm. October, 11am to 5pm
www.butterflycentre.co.uk

Facilities:
Shop, café, exhibition, video room

King Arthur's Labyrinth

Corris, Machynlleth, SY20 9RF
££

An enchanting visitor attraction for all the family, take a fascinating underground boat ride into the past, back to the times of King Arthur, through the great waterfall and into the dramatic caverns of the Labyrinth; deep, deep under the mountain! Hear the stories of King Arthur and other ancient legends unfold. You'll hear of mean giants, fearsome dragons, brave battles and much more. When back above ground, take time to explore the maze of Bard's Quest.

Opening Times:
Times vary throughout the year, please see website **www.kingarthurslabyrinth.com**

Facilities:
Guided tours, parking, shop, refreshments

Brecon Beacons National Park

Brecon, Powys

An ideal place for all ages to explore, take a picnic and enjoy the tranquillity and beauty of the surroundings. Spanning an incredible 519 miles, this famous country park won't disappoint you, nor will you forget its breathtaking scenery and expanse of lakes and greenery. Whether you want to take advantage of the surroundings and have a day of exploration, or just want to take your picnic and relax in awe of the scenery – this is a must-see part of the Land of Song! Llangorse Lake (below) is a great place to base yourself to explore the area.

www.breconbeacons.org
www.llangorselake.co.uk

Cardiff Castle

Castle Street, Cardiff, CF10 3RB

£££

Take a trip to this stunning castle and explore over 2,000 years of fascinating history! Within its Gothic towers there are lavish and luxurious dwellings rich with beautiful murals, Italian and Arabian décor, sparkling stained glass and impressive marble. The castle has lived through many ages, which is evident from its Roman Wall for viewing and the Norman keep, which visitors are able to climb. There are tours around the amazing Clock Tower on a daily basis.

Opening Times:
Daily except 25 December, 26 December and 1 January; March - October: 9am - 6pm (last tour 5pm); November - February: 9am - 5pm (last tour 4pm)
www.cardiffcastle.com

Facilities:
Disabled limited, shop, guided tours, café

Caldey Island

Off Tenby, SA70 7UJ

Easily reached by a boat trip from Tenby Harbour, Caldey Island is an exquisitely beautiful island for all ages to enjoy. Inhabited since as far back as the Stone Age, the island is home to monks from the Cistercian Order and you can attend one of the amazing chanted services in the Abbey Church. Children can play on the lovely sandy beaches; and you can take a walk up to the charming lighthouse, taking stock of the magnificent views of the surrounding coastal areas, such as Tenby, the Preseli Hills and Lundy Island. For a relaxing and peaceful trip out, Caldey Island is the place for you.

Opening Times:
Times vary throughout the year, please see website
www.caldey-island.co.uk

Facilities:
Disabled full, shop, refreshments

Colby Woodland Garden

Amroth, Narberth, Pembrokeshire, SA67 8PP
££

With plenty of woodland walks and pretty meadows to enjoy, this beautiful woodland garden takes its visitors through secluded valleys and along open and wooded pathways for a great trip out. The garden is famously known as one of the best collections of rhododendrons and azaleas in Wales. As well as the pleasant surroundings and walks, there are plenty of things to keep children amused, with safari packs and a children's quiz.

Opening Times:
For opening times, please see website for details in season
www.nationaltrust.org

Facilities:
Braille guide, dogs on leads welcome, shop, café

Portmeirion

Gwynedd, LL48 6ER, Wales

Portmeirion was built by Welsh architect Clough Williams-Ellis from 1925 to 1973. The Portmeirion estate includes 70 acres of sub-tropical woodlands, known as the Gwyllt, as well as farmland and the village itself on the southern side of its own private peninsula on the coast of Snowdonia.

Portmeirion is open every day of the year and provides hotel accommodation and self-catering accommodation in the cottages that make up the village. The village is also a popular visitor attraction, open daily all year from 09:30 to 17:30.

Check official website for details, **www.portmeirion-village.com**

Edinburgh Castle

Castle Hill, Edinburgh, EH1 2NG
£££ /Children under 5 – Free

Once the home of kings and queens, this world-famous and magnificent castle is one of Edinburgh's top tourist attractions. With lavish furniture and décor within the luxurious royal apartments and the stunning sight of the castle's Great Hall with its beautifully ornate ceiling and fine collection of weapons, visitors will be in no doubt that this castle was indeed a fitting regal residence. You can see the Scottish crown jewels, the Stone of Destiny and enjoy the popular Prisons of War experience, as well as see the fifteenth century siege canon, Mons Meg.

Opening Times:
March to September, 9.30am to 6pm.
October to March, 9.30am to 5pm
www.edinburghcastle.gov.uk

Facilities:
Disabled full, parking, tours, shop, café

Our Dynamic Earth

Holyrood Road, Edinburgh, EH8 8AS
£££

A fantastic journey of discovery taking you from the very beginning of time, right through to the future! With the dramatic special effects, you'll see the Big Bang, be shaken by volcanoes, swim in the oceans and enjoy a whole host of other physical and visual experiences centred in, around and across planet Earth! Look further into the world's concerns over climate change and discuss the issues in the Future Dome and marvel in this fun and informative attraction's state-of-the-art interactive exhibits and activities. So be 'Dynamic' and go along!

Opening Times:
Daily, 10am to 5pm (July & August 10am to 6pm)

Facilities:
Disabled full, parking, shop, café

www.dynamicearth.co.uk

Royal Observatory Visitor Centre

Blackford Hill, Edinburgh, EH9 3HJ
££

Open for pre-booked group visits and special events, this interactive and interesting centre is a welcome look into the mesmerising world of astronomy. Throughout your tour you'll see and hear about comets, the solar system, the changing seasons and get to handle rocks from outer space; there's also a collection of meteorites to see. The Astronomers will treat you to fascinating facts and information, as well as being happy to answer any questions you may have about the vast subject of the universe! The centre organises events throughout the year, such as a science festival and storytelling festival, please see website for further details.

Opening Times:
Times may vary, please see website for details **www.roe.ac.uk**

Facilities:
Guided tours, parking, shop

Museum of Childhood

42 High Street, Royal Mile, Edinburgh, EH1 1TG
Free

Holding precious memories of all things related to childhood, this is a trip into history of a very different kind! Holding nostalgia for adults and fascinating sights for children, the museum is dedicated to children and filled to the brim with childhood toys and games, past and present, from all over the world. The galleries range from teddy bears and dolls to train sets and tricycles. The exhibitions show how children dressed, played and learned and there's even footage of children filmed in 1951, playing street games in Edinburgh.

Opening Times:
Daily, Mon to Sat 10am to 5pm. Sun 12pm to 5pm **www.cac.org.uk**

Facilities:
Disabled full, shop

Museum of Transport

1 Bunhouse Road, Glasgow, G3 8DP
Free

Dedicated to the fascinating history of land and sea transport, exhibits include; horse-drawn carriages, railway engines, motorcycles, fire engines, motor cars, ship models and many more historically important items of interest. The museum takes its visitors back in time to a re-created 1938 Glasgow street, with the transport that would have travelled its streets; and there's also an authentically reconstructed underground station. Lovers of transport, big or small, will delight in the wide variety of vehicles and vessels on display.

Opening Times:
Daily, exc. 25 & 26 Dec. 1 & 2 Jan. Mon to Thurs 10am to 5pm. Fri & Thurs 11am to 5pm
www.glasgowmuseums.com

Facilities:
Disabled access, parking, guided tours, café, shop

Archaeolink Prehistory Park

Opyne, Insch, Aberdeenshire, AB52 6QP
££

Set in the stunning Aberdeenshire countryside, overlooked by the Bennachie mountain range, this multi award-winning history park will take you on a journey through 1,000 years of history, from the Mesolithic to a Roman Marching Camp. The unique indoor and outdoor archaeological exhibitions include guided tours, workshops and interactive activities for all to enjoy. The park is of great historical interest and children will enjoy its wonderfully inclusive focus on participation, fun and learning.

Opening Times:
Daily, April to October 10am to 5pm
www.archaeolink.co.uk

Facilities:
Disabled full, guided tours, shop, café, refreshments

Satrosphere

The Tramsheds, 179 Constitution Street, Aberdeen, AB24 5TU
££

An exciting world of fun and exploration for youngsters and grown-ups! This attraction is dedicated to finding out exactly how the world works and its interesting and interactive exhibits allow participation for all ages. Light up a plasma dome, look out into infinity, take part in the interactive shows and step inside a giant bubble. Get back to nature finding out all about food and farming, discover the fascinating world of slugs, snails and ants and get involved in a number of workshops and special events throughout the year.

Opening Times:
Please check website for details
www.satrosphere.net

Facilities:
Disabled access, shop, café

M & D's Theme Park

Strathcylde Country Park, Motherwell, ML1 3RT
Please see website for details

Situated in over 20 acres of the picturesque Strathclyde Country Park, this exciting theme park has over 40 rides and attractions, including a huge indoor family complex and 'Amazonia' a simulated indoor tropical rainforest, with animals and greenery familiar to this tropically heated habitat. There are white-knuckle rides such as The Tsunami, Tornado and The Express and family rides for younger children to enjoy; Big Apple, Flying Bees and Flying Jumbos! Enjoy the indoor bowling centre, with its 'Bowl n' Bite' restaurant and the authentic Italian coffee shop and delicious ice-cream parlour.

Opening Times:
Times and dates vary throughout the year, please see website for details
www.scotlandsthemepark.com

Facilities:
Disabled full, parking, shop, café

Nevis Range Mountain Experience

Nevis Range, Torlundy, Fort William, PH33 6SW

££

One of the Highlands most popular visitor attractions, Nevis Range is enveloped by some of the world's most breathtaking and ancient landscapes. A real joy for all the family to experience, take a unique trip up on Britain's only mountain gondola up to 120ft and be awe inspired by the magnificent views over the West Highlands. Visitors to the range can opt to ski or snowboard in the vast surroundings, or to access the exceptional climbing opportunities. There are even bike trails to suit everyone from seasoned racers to families!

Opening Times: *Daily, 10am to 5pm. Events may change times, please see website for details* **www.nevisrange.co.uk**

Facilities: *Disabled full, parking, shop, café, refreshments*

Jedforest Deer and Farm Park

Mervinslaw Estate, Jedburgh, TD8 8PL

££/Children under 5 - Free

A great day out for all the family, this modern day working farm has all the sights, sounds and smells of the beautiful Scottish countryside. Set amongst hills, streams and woods; you'll be treated to seeing deer herds, including rare breeds and a wide range of farm animals. The park's attractions include Ranger-led activities and scenic walks, nature trails, pony rides and birds of prey displays.

Opening Times: *Easter – August 10am to 5.30pm, September – October 11am to 4.30pm* **www.jedforestdeerpark.co.uk**

Facilities: *Disabled access, parking, shop, café*

The Wheel of Belfast

City Hall, Belfast
££/Children under 4 – Free

After its arrival in the heart of Belfast in October 2007, this spectacular 60m wheel has fast become a popular tourist attraction. Located in the grounds of the City Hall, visitors can board the wheel's 'gondolas', (which are fully heated and air conditioned), and take a 15 minute slow-ride to take in the stunning views.

Opening Times:
Sun to Thurs, 10am to 9pm. Fri, 10am to 10pm. Sat, 9am to 10pm.
www.worldtouristattractions.co.uk

Facilities:
Disabled access – please note that door width is 74cm.

Aunt Sandra's Candy Factory

60 Castlereagh Road, Belfast, BT5 5FP
Please see website for details

Step back in time to the 1950's at Aunt Sandra's and be treated to a treasure trove of colour, candy and confectionery! This unique factory produces the most scrumptious selection of candy, boiled sweets, chocolate, fudge and many, many recipes spanning back over 100 years. Tours around the factory run daily, watch how the candy is hand-made with its authentic 1950's equipment and enjoy the fantastic wares to be sampled!

Opening Times:
Mon to Fri, 9.30am to 5pm, Sat, 10am to 4.30pm **www.irishcandyfactory.com**

W5 Online

Odyssey, 2 Queen's Quay, Belfast, BT3 9QQ
££

Ireland's first discovery centre of its kind, this award-winning interactive attraction will tease your senses, stretch your imagination and stimulate your brain with exhibits dedicated to providing hours of fun and exploration into the world of science. See Dino Jaw or come and assemble a wind powered car and race it at one of the centre's special exhibitions. For special events, please check the website.

Opening Times:
School term: Mon to Thurs 10am to 5pm, Fri & Sat 10am to 6pm, Sun 12pm to 6pm. School holidays, 10am to 6pm.
www.w5online.co.uk

Facilities:
Parking, shop, café, refreshments

Belfast Zoo

Antrim Road, Belfast, BT36 7PN
£££

Set against the backdrop of Cave Hill, the zoo is home to more than 1,200 animals and 140 species. The majority of the animals are endangered species and the zoo offers vast enclosures and beautiful habitats. Come and see the magnificent white tiger, Barbary lions, giraffes, elephants, bongos, tapirs, gorillas and much more. Rainforest House is a tropical walk-through exhibition with beautiful landscaping and amazing animals.

Opening Times:
Daily; March to September, 10am to 7pm. October to March 10am to 4pm
www.belfastzoo.co.uk

Facilities:
Disabled full, parking, café, refreshments, restaurant, shop

Bluelough Adventure Centre

The Grange Courtyard, Castlewellan Forest Park, Castlewellan, County Down
Please see website for details

For all activities relating to mountain and water sports, Bluelough is a great day out! Set in the Mourne Mountains, the centre hosts a wealth of activities include; rock climbing, abseiling, canoeing, archery, kayaking, hill walking, orienteering, raft building and lots more. All the activities are aimed at all levels of experience and provide coaching for beginners. For a full list of activities and events, please see the website.

Opening Times:
Times and dates vary, please see website
www.mountainandwater.com

Facilities:
Café, shop, equipment hire, showers

Carnfunnock Country Park

Coast Road, Larne, BT40 2QG
Please see website for details

Boasting stunning panoramic views of the Antrim Coast and North Channel, this park is full of thrilling attractions. With woodland and colour-rich gardens, walking trails and coastline there's time to relax and wind down as children have fun with the other attractions and entertainment. There is an outdoor adventure playground, mini golf area, bouncy castle, activity centre and much more.

Opening Times:
All year, except 25 Dec & 1 Jan. July & August, 9am to 9pm. All other times, 9am to dusk. Attractions are seasonal.
www.carnfunnock.com

Facilities:
Disabled full, parking, shop, café

Saint Patrick's Trian Visitor Complex

40 English Street, Armagh
££

With exhibitions, games and crafts to keep the whole family amused, this complex consists of three main attraction areas; firstly there's the Land of Lilliput, where the famous work 'Gulliver's Travels' is read to children, with the help of a 20ft giant! Secondly there's Saint Patrick's Testament – The Book of Armagh, dedicated to learning about the ancient manuscript; and thirdly, The Armagh Story, an opportunity to step back in time and visit historic Armagh.

Opening Times:
Please see website for details
www.saintpatrickstrian.com

Facilities:
Shop, restaurant, parking

Carrick-a-Rede Rope Bridge
119a White Park Road, Ballintoy, Ballycastle, Co. Antrim BT54 6LS
££/Check wesbite for further details

One of Northern Ireland's best-loved attractions in an area of outstanding natural beauty, this is an exhilarating coastal path experience with visitors drawn to the rope bridge challenge! Once you reach Carrick Island, the reward is seeing the diverse birdlife and an uninterrupted view across to Rathlin Island and Scotland. There is only one way off the island - back across the swinging bridge! Don't look down!

Opening Times: *Bridge open, weather permitting; 1 Mar-25 May: 10am-6pm daily, 26 May- 31 Aug : 10am-7pm daily, 1 Sep- 2 Nov: 10am-6pm daily* **www.nationaltrust.org.uk**

Facilities: *Refreshments, guided tours, picnic area, disabled access, car park*

Giant's Causeway
44a Causeway Road, Bushmills, Co. Antrim BT57 8SU
Free/donations welcome

The legendary emblem of North Antrim's spectacular coastline, no visit to Northern Ireland is complete without a visit to the Giant's Causeway. An area of outstanding natural and mythological beauty with fabulous flora and fauna, it is Northern Ireland's only World Heritage Site.

Opening Times: *Daily*

Facilities: *Refreshments, picnic area, shop, car park*